A BRIXHAM A

Compiled by the Brixham Museum and History Society
with the help of Chips Barber

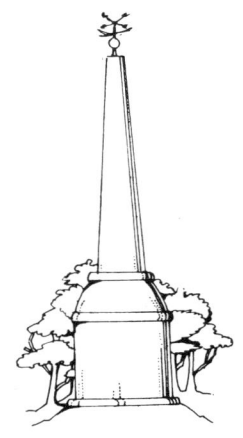

Obelisk Publications

Other Books in this Series

Albert Labbett's Crediton Collection
Albert Labbett's Crediton Collection II
An Alphington Album, *P. Aplin & J. Gaskell*
The Dawlish Collection, *Bernard Chapman*
The Totnes Collection, *Bill Bennett*
Peter Tully's Pictures of Paignton
Peter Tully's Pictures of Paignton Part II
Ian Jubb's Exeter Collection
Mike & Hilary Wreford's Okehampton Collection
Mike & Hilary Wreford's Okehampton Collection II
Fred Tozer's Newton Abbot Album
Pictorial Torquay, *Leslie Retallick*
Kingsteignton Collection, *Richard Harris*
A Chudleigh Collection
An Exeter Boyhood, *Frank Retter*
Dartmoor in Colour, *Chips Barber*
Beautiful Exeter, *Chips Barber*
Torbay in Colour, *Chips Barber*
Plymouth in Colour, *Chips Barber*

For further details of these or any of our extensive Devon titles, please contact us at 2 Church Hill, Pinhoe, Exeter, EX4 9ER, Tel: (0392) 468556.

Some Other Obelisk Publications

Diary of a Dartmoor Walker, *Chips Barber*
Diary of a Devonshire Walker, *Chips Barber*
Under Sail Thr S Devon & Dartmoor, *R. B. Cattell*
The Great Little Dartmoor Book, *Chips Barber*
Made in Devon, *Chips Barber and David FitzGerald*
Tales of the Unexplained in Devon, *Judy Chard*
Haunted Happenings in Devon, *Judy Chard*
Tales of the Teign, *Chips Barber and Judy Chard*
The Ghosts of Torbay, *Deryck Seymour*
The Ghosts of Totnes, *Bob Mann*
The Ghosts of Brixham, *Graham Wyley*
The Great Little Totnes Book, *Chips Barber*
Ten Family Walks on Dartmoor, *Sally & Chips Barber*
Torquay / Paignton / Brixham, *Chips Barber*
The Templer Way, *Derek Beavis*
The Magic Triangle, *Deryck Seymour*
The Secret Circle, *Deryck Seymour*
Boat Trip Down the Dart, *Bob Mann*
Walking with a Tired Terrier in and Around Torbay, *Brian Carter*
Torquay United – the First 70 Years, *Laura Joint*
Cockington, *Jo Connell*

First Published in 1994 by Obelisk Publications
2 Church Hill, Pinhoe, Exeter, Devon
Designed by Chips and Sally Barber
Typeset by Sally Barber
Printed in Great Britain by
Ashley House, Marsh Barton, Exeter

© Obelisk Publications 1994
All Rights Reserved

Acknowledgements

Thanks to all the unknown photographers and sources whose works are included in this book. Special thanks to Mr Derek Wilson and Mr Ivan Parton for all their invaluable research and involvement.

ISBN: 0 946651 90 6

This is a collection of photographs of Brixham that features events, people and places. Since these pictures were taken changes have occurred, some obvious, others more subtle. We hope that you will enjoy this nostalgic stroll along "Memory Lane."
The above photo is from about 1950 when the people of Brixham filled the streets with a carnival atmosphere. The policeman is PC Banks.

Brixham has grown in a deep, steep valley. In this print of about 1849 the Admiralty reservoir is clearly shown. The Town Hall now stands on this spot. In the right hand foreground the Assembly Rooms can be seen. These were built in 1835 at the bottom of Bolton Street. Behind these is the Methodist Chapel in Fore Street having been built some nineteen years earlier, in 1816. In the background is The Breakwater, begun in 1843, and only half its present length in this drawing.

Milton Street is the main approach road into Brixham from the Kingswear direction. Its name derives from one of the three defensive farms set up against Saxon invaders. These were Upton, Middleton and Lowerton (alias Lupton). The first and last became hamlets, now absorbed into Brixham but Middleton only survives, in a corrupted form, in Milton Street. In this photo Milton Farm, now nos. 111 and 113 Milton Street, can be seen left of centre. The house on the front left has been demolished.

Quite a crowd have gathered to witness the fire brigade assembled for a photograph. The picture was taken outside Jabez Lake's house at the bottom of Rea Barn. The cottage on the right is still there but this big house was pulled down in about 1928.

This row of cottages stood at the top of Bolton Street just below Rea Barn Quarry. They were known as 'Fried Taddy Row' because of the smell of chips that were cooked all day long by Granny Williams. These cottages were demolished in 1928 as part of the road widening of the Great Gate road junction.

During both World Wars there were many Belgian families living in Brixham. They were soon integrated into the local community and many even stayed on after the cessation of hostilities. During the Second World War they had their own club which was located in Burton Street. There were also a number of Free French people in the town, who had their club in Fore Street. This fine photograph shows a joint Free French/Belgian procession, in 1943, going down Fore Street. They are preceeded by the band from the British Seaman's Home in Brixham. Their HQ and home was in Berry Head Road and in the many years that it existed many hundreds of young boys passed through it. Today it is a centre for water-based pursuits.

The picture on the opposite page is of the Torbay Paint Works in New Road. The enterprise was started in the 1840s by Samuel Calley and Richard Wolston. Both of them owned mines in the Brixham area from which ochre was extracted. This was an important ingredient in a type of paint that possessed anti-corrosion properties. The manufactured product was distributed all over the world and was used particularly in the paint coating of iron structures, bridges and ships. The firm changed hands just before the end of the nineteenth century being bought by Stevens and Co. This company, in turn, was bought out by Pinchin Johnson and Associates in 1925. In the Second World War 'Torbay Paints' produced some three million gallons of camouflage paint for military installations. In 1960 the company was bought by Courtaulds and it was announced that the paint works would close down the following year — 1961. Since then the buildings on the site have been used for a range of light industries.

9

The building above once stood on Rea Barn Hill but has been demolished for road widening purposes and for land for council houses across from the police station. The two pictures on the opposite page give a hint that Brixham is a town of steep hills. The one on the left shows Broad Steps, as they looked in about 1930, looking up Higher Street. The house on the right was demolished shortly afterwards. The property glimpsed at the top is known as Shotover Cottages and was once the site of the Shotover Inn.

The far picture on the right is of Middle Street and shows the house where William of Orange is reputed to have stayed the night after his landing at Brixham on 5 November 1688. To the right of it is Mill Tye Steps that lead down to Pump Street. The name of these steps commemorates the watermill that once stood near this point. It was driven by water carried in leats from Laywell, in Milton Street, and from Lupton via New Road. Mr Blackler had a shop near these steps until he moved to the opposite side.

11

One of the problems facing photographers at Brixham is that the narrow streets, with tall buildings, tend to be shadowy. This view of Middle Street is a good example. This picture was taken in 1958 and the road has since been widened, all the properties on the left having been demolished. The right side remains as shown in the photo.

This is how the eastern end of Fore Street looked in about 1900. The buildings on the left, known locally as 'The Island', were demolished in the course of road widening in 1908/09. Lloyds Bank is now on this site at the corner of Pump Street. Just about discernible is the clock on the wall of the Brixham Co-operative Society. This business was founded in 1890 and its original premises were in St Peter's Hill.

13

Here we have two very different views of Fore Street, Brixham's main shopping street. On this page we see its western end with the gabled roof of the old Methodist Sunday School on the left. This was built, in 1889, at a cost of £2,000 but was replaced, in 1975, by the present Christian Community Centre. There used to be two cinemas in this part of Fore Street, The Electric and The Regent. However both of these picture palaces had closed by 1966.

The photograph on the opposite page is the eastern end of Fore Street and shows a mixture of transport types with a horse and wagon on the left and more 'modern' horseless carriages on the right!

FORE STREET BRIXHAM.

Here is a view looking from Market Street up Church Hill. The building in the top right corner of the photograph is now the Smugglers Haunt Hotel. For many years this was Mr Cooksley's workshop and beside it was a dairy. On the left is Pring's Court which was known at an earlier date as Pomeroy's Court. Nos 3 and 4 are dated 1783 and the houses are reputed to have been the lodgings of some of the officers attached to the Berry Head forts. The sea-faring Pring family lived there in the second half of the nineteenth century. The two buildings in the middle of the picture and the front-walled garden have now been replaced by a shop and a store. One was occupied by Mrs Loveridge who tempted her young customers with her delicious home-made sweets.

The opposite picture is taken just a stone's throw away. It shows Bolton Cross, or Market Cross as it was then known before the advent of the motor car. 'Bolton' appears here with regularity – Bolton Cross, Bolton Street and the Bolton Hotel all derive their names from The Duke of Bolton, once a hereditary Lord of the Manor of Brixham. Queen Victoria's Diamond Jubilee (1897) was commemorated by the fountain erected on the corner of Market Street. It has since been demolished, its base forming part of the wishing well that was placed on Eastern Quay – but is now missing. Would the good lady have been amused?

17

On these two pages we have an easily identifiable pair of photos, one almost being the reverse view of the other. The Admiralty Reservoir, referred to already on page 4, had become disused by 1882 and the land where it was had become the private property of H. W. Nelson of London. He kindly gave the land to the town so that a much needed Public Hall and Market could be built. This fine public building, of limestone,

18

and shown on the left, was opened on 1 October 1886 and cost between £3-4,000 to build. The architect was George Bridgman who was also the designer of the original Oldway Mansion at Paignton.

The Cottage Hospital and District Nursing Institute, in Cavern Hill, was opened on 25 March 1894. It cost £1,500 and was given to the town by Miss A. M. C. Hogg (grand-daughter of the Rev Henry Francis Lyte). She subsequently became the superintendent of the hospital. It stayed in use until 1928 when it was replaced by the present one in Greenswood Road.
The photograph on top of the opposite page shows rescue work being undertaken during the floods of 1947. Houses in Kingswear and Brixham were inundated by waters that rose to a depth of over eight feet. The bus, in the lower photo, is at the bottom of Bolton Street.

21

How many memories will be rekindled by the sight of this fleet of motor coaches and buses belonging to 'Burton Cars'? This firm, owned by John Geddes, began operating in 1925 and originally only ran in the summer. A lot of local people will have been on day trips and outings with this firm, which operated from this depot in Bolton Street. This photo was taken in 1955 from an adjacent roof top. Opposite would have been 'Fried Taddy Row', already referred to on page 7. There were other coach operators in Brixham. There were Mills (with The Bluebird) and Prouts of Churston. The competition from nearby Paignton included Gould and Sanders who ran 'The Paigntonian' and Coopers who ran 'Dandy Cars'.

22

There are many limestone quarries in the Brixham area, many now disused. This is Freshwater Quarry just around the corner from Brixham Harbour. The caption on the original photograph stated that this was a free car park but that is not the case today.

Taken from the heights of Furzeham this photograph presents a fine view across the harbour. Although this picture is easily recognisable from the buildings and features in it, so much has been added to the scene in the many decades since it was taken. Brixham has grown apace

and what were open spaces, in this picture, are now built up. Such is progress. Shoalstone and the coastguard cottages can be seen on the left of this photograph, which includes most of the length of Berry Head Road.

THE EMBANKMENT (STRAND) BRIXHAM 1889

It's strange how names can change with usage. The harbour side now known as The Strand was once known as The Beach. This photo dates back over a century to 1889. The retaining walls and roadway that are there today were built in 1897 in the Diamond Jubilee year of the reign of Queen Victoria. Therefore it is no surprise to discover that it was named The Victoria Embankment. In the course of the construction the slipway was realigned and moved further from the statue of William of Orange.

26

The presence of the 'modern' motor vehicles on The Strand is evidence that this photograph is taken a lot later than the one on the opposite page. Had this picture been in colour it would have revealed that the great majority of houses overlooking the harbour would have been painted in drab colours, unlike today when this hillside is adorned with a multi-coloured variety of properties.

28

Brixham is a bride of the sea and almost everything that went on here at one time had something to do with it. To the right are three men at work in a barking yard. In such places special tanning agents were applied to sails to preserve them. Each yard had their own special formula but the principal raw material was powdered oak bark. Other constituents included ochre, tallow, linseed oil and water. These were all boiled up in a cauldron, a truly potent mix! The yards were merely a clear space where the sails could be laid out flat for treatment and a tall spar with block and tackle was on site to hoist them up for drying. In Brixham there were two such barking yards, one in Overgang and one on Southern Quay.

The picture on the far left shows the Fish Market on The Quay as it would have appeared six days of the week. It was customary to lay the catch out singly so that intending purchasers could satisfy themselves that poor quality fish was not being hidden under the good. Until 1870 it was the fisher women who did the selling. They did this by means of a Dutch Auction. In this system the auctioneer calls out the highest price thought appropriate and then progressively reduces it until a buyer is found.

The other picture on the opposite page needs little explanation but is one that has been popular with postcard manufacturers as it has a sense of presence about it and conveys the past atmosphere of this old fishing port. It features Mr Matthews in Mill Tye, mending nets.

In this photograph Harry Mills is shown with the happy smiling faces of Mrs Foale, Mrs Rogers, Mrs Seaward and Mrs Green. The task they are performing is 'rodding' the sprats. The photograph is taken at the old stables in Middle Street in the 1950s.

The Fish Market, Brixham   CDS26313   Chapman and Son, Dawlish

There were more postcards of this type in the past, this one having been taken by the famous firm of Chapman and Son of Dawlish. Brixham was a fishing port and the postcard manufacturers went to great lengths to reflect this. A scene like this was far more effective, in black and white, than a view. In this 1950s' picture the men are winging ray.

31

In the above picture a group of fishermen have assembled for a photograph. They are a mixture of boys and men, the latter with faces hardened by years of going to sea in all weathers. All of them are wearing caps and most are dressed in fishermen's jerseys, all part and parcel of life in a profession where losses at sea were frequent and times invariably tough.

On the opposite page is a splendid photo of a sawpit where timber is being prepared for use in shipbuilding. The man on top was the senior man and decided how and where the log was to be cut. He then, expertly, guided the saw to his marks. The pit, itself, was dug in the ground and lined with planking. The log about to be cut was supported on cross timbers that were moved along as the sawing progressed. The steam logsaw was invented in 1845 and by 1880 most shipyards were using them. However here it is still a manual job, one that attracted many spectators.

33

This picture was taken about 1900 and shows the Cachalot on the stocks at Dewdney's Yard which was at the South Quay.

Freshwater Quarry survived in operation until 1927 and when it closed the Urban District Council arranged for a connecting path to be built between it and Bench Quarry. The path also linked with Battery Gardens and Fishcombe and was duly and appropriately called the Marine Parade. This photo is of the quarry when it was being worked in August 1911 with the cut stone being loaded, by crane, onto awaiting ships. The quarry was briefly reopened when repairs were made to the Breakwater in 1933.

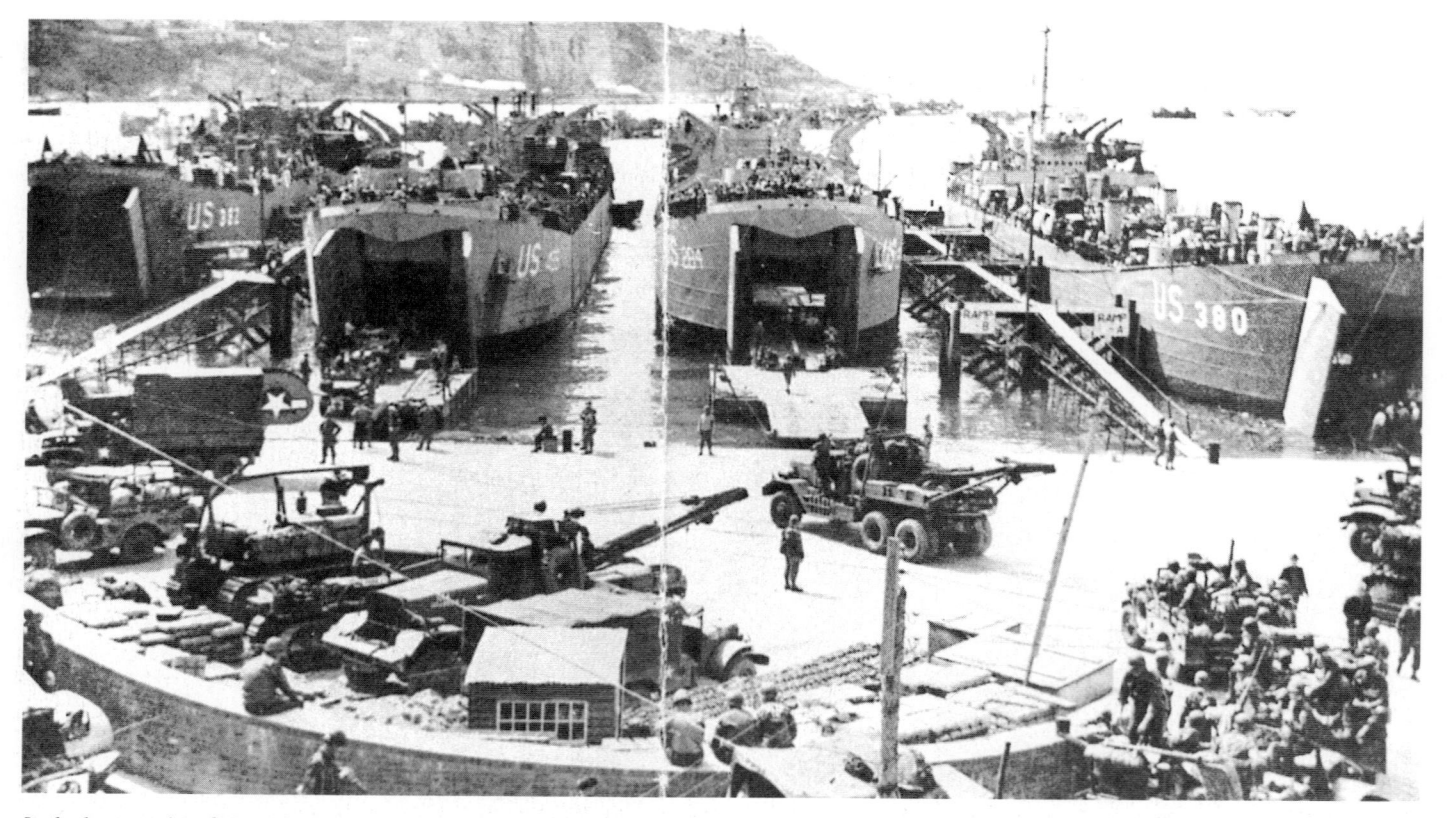

In the last weeks of May 1944 ports along the south coast of England were jammed as men and equipment were loaded onto boats and barges for the D-Day attack on France. The picture shows stores, troops and vehicles going aboard three Landing Craft Tanks (LCTs) at Brixham. The present Breakwater Hard was specially laid down at that time to facilitate the loading of shallow-draught boats.

The picture opposite shows one of three houses, in Berry Head Road, which were demolished in order to make the necessary access to The Breakwater for the D-Day preparations. They were requisitioned and pulled down to allow turning space for arriving vehicles. The work was ordered by The United States Combined Operations staff. In 1968, on the death of Sir Winston Churchill, gardens were opened on this site and named in honour of him.

37

Breakwater Beach doesn't look exactly like this any more even though the picture of it is instantly recognisable despite the passing of the years. It is a beach that is close enough to Brixham's harbour to attract people who don't mind a short stroll to it. It is sheltered from the prevailing south westerly winds and can be a veritable sun trap.

The Berry Head Cafe was not on Berry Head but in Berry Head Road! Here we have a large group of people assembled in front of it for the obligatory photograph. They are, in the main, stood very still but some are restless and their movement has resulted in some blurred expressions, a hazard when posing for a long exposure. The occasion was a celebration high tea for residents, of over seventy years of age, for the Silver Jubilee of George V in May 1935. The cafe was obviously an important and good sized venue for events as many other gatherings were held there.

One such gathering occurred on 5 July 1938. Shown here are delegates of the Grand Orange Lodge of England at a reception held to mark the 250th anniversary of William of Orange's landing at Brixham. The Berry Head Cafe could accommodate up to 250 people for a sit down meal and boasted in their advert, which appeared in local guides, that 350 more people could be catered for on the laid out lawns overlooking Shoalstone Beach. Inside a 'panatrope' played music for the Tuesday and Friday evening dances that were held there. The cafe served fresh lobster teas, and also cream teas but was demolished about 1950. Flats now stand on its former site.
The picture on the opposite page is of the obelisk, with its lantern, which commemorates that historic landing of William of Orange. Incorporated into it is the stone where William is said to have taken his first step on these shores. It has been moved about with alarming regularity having occupied many sites. In 1988, as part of the tercentenary celebrations, it was moved back to its original spot beside the old Fish Market on the Eastern Quay.

41

42

Brixham was once part of that great network of railways that embraced almost every town and village in the kingdom. Although it is an obvious statement to make, the station stood at the top of Station Hill, but there is little evidence of its former glory. Occasionally visitors come to make a pilgrimage to it and one man who came from Perth, in Western Australia, even has a large model of it that he made from a plan of the station lay-out and photographs. Not many Brixham folk will get the opportunity to feast their eyes on it so these photos will have to suffice. The railway line opened in 1868 and it was almost entirely through the efforts of business entrepreneur, Richard Wolston that the two mile long line to Churston came into being. The railway gave a tremendous boost to the economy of the town. Fish could now be taken to the great Billingsgate market in London in under seven hours! The coming of the railway also stimulated shipbuilding and many other ancillary trades. The original engine was called the "Queen" and the pub at the top of Station Hill is named in commemoration of her. This locomotive gave way to others all of which gave good service until the line closed in 1963.
On the top of the opposite page is the Brixham train waiting to leave Churston Station. The train was Locomotive 1470, a detail that would interest enthusiasts. The bottom photo is taken along this short branch line and shows Engine 1439 at Churston Court Farm in November 1951. On this page part of the platform of Brixham Station can be seen on the right side of the picture. It is surprising how this scene has changed so much since the branch line's demise. Bearing in mind the problems of summer traffic and the limited amount of car parking in the town this little line could have been a useful alternative, linked to a 'park and ride', had it been kept. But it is always easier to be wise after the event...

But towns are not just about buildings they are also about people and in Brixham, in the past, there was a strong feeling of community and a genuine sense of belonging. This last run of pictures should stir a few memories for people with a long association with the town. Here is the Brixham Youth Club of 1946 at their annual supper and social. We are reliably informed that the following individuals are amongst the gathered throng: Dennis Lovell, Peter Ingram, Bill Porter, Wilf Piper, Cyril Lawrence, Lillian Twyman, Dan Thomas, Bert Loram, Joan Tooley, R. Hannaford, Henry German, Ernie Ash, Ruby Pocock, Irma Davey, Celia Morris, Ruby Dick, Ted Baker, Ruby Dickinson, Mrs Bond (x2) George Cummings, Harry King, Miss Warren, Margaret Elliot, Roy Dumbleton, Bill Youlden, Mr Westaway, the Vicar and Jean Parnell.

Brixham Rugby Football club formed in 1875. In the early days the team turned out in 'guernsey frocks and white stockings' and became known as the 'Fishermen', the nickname has remained to this day. Their home ground is at Astley Park. The 1985/86 season team lines up as follows: (L to R) standing: David Wiggings (Coach), Robert Dart (Committee), John Huish (Manager), Graham Wood, John Lovell, Bob Houston, Keith Gardners, Peter McIntyre, Paul White, Terry Maggs, Barry Young, Andrew Hendy, Chris Ward, James Irvine, Adrian Taylor, Steve Wright, Tom Davies, Roger Morley (Manager), Trevor Harvey (Referee). Front: David Kay, John Farley, Simon Butterworth, Richard Dalton, Alec Richardson (President), Sean Irvine (Captain), Mike Linsdell (Chairman), Mark Faulkner, Glyn Jenkins, Alan Davies, Ian Griffin.

45

There was mention of a cricket team in Brixham in 1855 when a fete was held on Furzeham Green to commemorate the Fall of Sebastopol during the Crimean War. Since those days Brixham cricketers have played on Galmpton Warborough and Astley Park before finally making North Fields Lane their home ground. This Brixham team shows (L to R) back: D Buley (umpire), P. England, W. S. Harvey, E. M. Upham, E. G. A. Nolan. Front: R. Langford, P. Musgrove, F. A. Crang, T. A. Harper, G. J. Bright, E. W. B. Thomas. The photo was taken on 23 June 1963.

The first record of Association Football in Brixham was in 1904 when local enthusiasts met in Doidges Temperance Hotel in Fore Street to form a club. They played on Furzeham Green. The other soccer clubs are Brixham United and Brixham Town. This photograph is of the Herald Cup winning Brixham Villa side of the 1967/68 season. (L to R) Gordon Preston, John Mosedale, Alan Carter, Dave Maunder (Hidden), Bill Harris, Eric Coysh, Ian Alexander, Barry Mitcheson (with cup), Jill Bowles (mascot), Bill Loram, Dave Farley, Dave Hazlewood, Brian Burnell. They were the first Brixham team to win this trophy in a season when they also won the South Devon Premier League title.

Since this photograph was taken in 1905, millions of visitors have promenaded around this corner of the harbour happily snapping away to record their own visit and their own particular memories of their time in Brixham. It's appropriate that we should end here as it is a view that is essentially Brixham, a place that is a part of the larger administrative district of Torbay but a place with a very special atmosphere of its own. On the left is the Old Market House, built in 1799 and closed when the new Town Hall was constructed in 1886. As we have seen in this selection of old pictures life, even in Brixham, goes on changing, sometimes for the better but often for the worse. We hope you have enjoyed this nostalgic look at our town through these old pictures. Just remember if you want to see and share more of Brixham's past, then we are always pleased to see you down at the museum!